Le

to

"Har'poo"

Waiting on God
with Hope and Expectation

Ana Kerner

LEARNING TO "HAR'POO"

Waiting on God with Hope and Expectation

ISBN-10: 1530628636
ISBN-13: 978-1530628636

Cover design by Ana Kerner

The following were referred to for Bible quotations:

The Holy Bible in Hebrew and English, Copyright 2014 The Bible Society in Israel

The Scriptures, Copyright 2012 by the Institute for Scripture Research, South Africa

Langenscheidt Pocket Hebrew Dictionary to the Old Testament, Hebrew English, by Dr. Karl Feyerabend, Printed in Germany

Student's Hebrew and Chaldee Dictionary to the Old Testament, compiled by Alexander Harkavy, Hebrew Publishing Company, New York, 1914

Buy My Books At: www.amazon.com

Contact Me At: annsart29@gmail.com

DEDICATION

This book is dedicated to my friend Maria.

Maria often calls to ask me to look up Scripture in my Hebrew Bible in order to see if the Hebrew words make a difference in the understanding of the verses.

About a year ago she called me up one night and said she had been reading Psalm 46. She wanted to know what the Hebrew word for "Be still" was in verse 10.

IT IS THE HEBREW WORD, "HAR'POO".

FORWARD

"Then YHWH (the Lord) said…

*The vision is yet
for an appointed time.*

*It is hastening towards the goal
and it will not fail.*

*Though it may be slow in coming,
WAIT for it,
for it certainly will come,
it will not delay!"*

Habakkuk 2:2&3

My life has been a life of *"learning to har'poo"*. This is not an easy or natural thing to learn. It takes focus and effort. But the result is being able to withstand severe stress and pressure with strength, peace and even joy.

The essence of *"learning to har'poo"* is acquiring the ability to see the world and individual circumstances through the "eyes of God", our Almighty Creator, knowing He is in control of all things, that whatever you are going through right now has been allowed by Him, and because He has allowed it, it is for your ultimate good. It has purpose.

"Har'poo" is the word that is translated, in Psalm 46, as "*be still*...and know that I am God".

To do this we must TRULY trust Almighty God, in

His goodness and in His greatness.

I know, from my many experiences that learning to *"har'poo"* opens the door for miracles to happen!

When we try to accomplish on our own what only God can do, we block God's miracles. We can ONLY do the natural, but God can and does, the SUPER. If we want to experience the SUPER-natural we must *"har'poo"* and watch God work His miracles!

Many of the miracles I have experienced in my own life are in my book, "If God Can Use Me, He Can Certainly Use You Too!" I wrote this book to be an encouragement to ANYONE!

Here's a shortened list:

My own healing from a severe head injury at age 14 (the complete healing took 46 yrs!)

Witnessing God "multiply" my 50 Russian Bibles into 2,700 in 5 days and be flown into Russia!

Being in the right place at the right time to help save the lives of 2 of my grandchildren.

How God used me and my experiences from my own head injury to help "pull" another one of my grandsons out of AUTISM.

And the list goes on…

Now, go back and re-read the Scripture verses in Habakkuk 2:2&3. Pray about what you are going through. Ask God to give you HIS vision for your current situation.

It is my prayer that this current book will be an inspiration to you so you will also experience the miracles God has for YOU and that through them He will be glorified!

CONTENTS

IMPATIENCE IS NATURAL

"See how the farmer waits
for the precious fruit of the earth
and is patient with it
until it receives the early and the latter rains.
So also,
you must be patient..."

James 5:7&8

People are naturally impatient.

Why?

The answer is simple. We want results NOW. We want gratification NOW. We want healing NOW. We want prosperity NOW. We want everything OUR way in OUR time.

And we do not want to suffer. Oftentimes patience involves a degree of "suffering", or so we think.

This may shock you but impatience is actually born out of a "self" centered focus. This is why it is natural. Everyone is born with a tendency to think of "self" as the center of life.

True patience can only come when we get our eyes off ourselves and onto God.

The key to acquiring patience and waiting on God is to change our thinking. Simple, but not easy to do.

First, lets look at the example of the farmer in the Scripture above.

A farmer plants seeds. Actually, before the farmer can

even plant the seeds he must prepare the soil.

Think of the soil as the condition of your mind and heart. Do you have clean fertile *"ground"* there? Or does some work need to be done? Do you have rocks to be cleared out? Do you have weeds to be pulled? Do you have thorn bushes that need to be dug up and burned?

*"You visit the earth (your heart and mind) and water it,
You greatly enrich it;
The river of Elohim (God) is filled with water;
You provide the grain,
for so You have prepared it.*

*The ridges have been filled,
the furrows have been deepened.*

*You make it soft with showers,
You bless its growth.*

*You have crowned the year with Your goodness,
and Your paths drip with fatness.*

*The pastures of the wilderness drip,
and the hills are filled with rejoicing.
The fields are full of flocks,
and the valleys are covered with grain.*

They shout for joy and sing!"

Psalm 65:9-13

There is a process from preparing the ground to the harvest. If the ground is not prepared well, if it is not planted with good seed, if it is not watered properly, there will not be an abundant harvest.

Farmers understand patience. Farmers understand what it means to wait.

In the first line of the Scripture above I put in parenthesis *(your heart and mind)*. I did this because I like to think of these verses as referring to **your heart and mind!**

Becoming a patient person, one who can wait on God, requires a change of heart and mind!

Back to the farmer.

Once the farmer clears the ground of rocks, weeds, thorns and every type of garbage, he is ready to enrich the soil.

How do you clear the **ground** of your heart and mind?

I suggest doing a project on yourself. Ask God what is in your heart and mind that should not be there? Make a list on one side of a page of paper. This will be an ongoing list as God reveals things to you. Now, on the other side of the paper write down what God would like to transform those negative qualities into.

For example, **Anger** can be transformed into **Dying to Self**. **Hate** can be transformed into **Acceptance**. **Fear** can be transformed into **Bold Trust** and **Confidence in God**. And so on...

These are only examples from when I did this project with the help of God. He would reveal things to me that I didn't even realize were there.

The same will be true for you.

After you start the list, I believe part of your success will lie in understanding the **root cause** of each negative

3

character quality and or emotion. Ask God to reveal these to you. You need to understand the source in order to **dig out the root cause.**

Don't fall into blame at this point! We must all take responsibility for where we are right now and trust God to meet us there. God can and will bring beauty from the ashes of our lives and experiences if we let Him.

We have ALL been hurt by others. But we have a choice. We can stay "stuck" in our pain and become bitter and resentful, OR we can "take a leap of faith" and let God redeem our pain. We can learn from others mistakes as well as our own. In fact, it is preferable to not have to go through the process of learning from our own mistakes. Wisdom is learning by observing the mistakes other people have made and, with God's help, avoid making those same mistakes.

Once you are on the path of cleaning up your heart and mind you can go on to the next step...*enriching the soil as you go on*.

How do you *enrich the soil* of your heart and mind?

Enrichment comes first, by reading Scripture and prayer. And not just a little, a lot.

I think one of the biggest problems with people who have faith in God is that most have never read the whole Bible for themselves! This has major consequences in a person's life.

It is not enough just to listen to preachers or to your pastor give a sermon once a week. You don't eat just once a week. You normally eat three meals a day and maybe in between too! If your body needs regular, daily food, what about your soul? Once a week nourishment will not, not, not, be enough to nourish your heart and mind!

Maybe many people don't read the whole Bible for

themselves because they feel it's intimidating, the Bible is a big book!

Here is a suggestion.

Get a Bible translation you are comfortable with. Then get a Bible marking pen. Bible marking pens won't bleed through onto the other side so they are worth getting.

Now, start reading in Genesis, marking every verse that has meaning to you. Special meaning. After Genesis, either go on to Exodus or pick another book of the Bible that interests you. Start reading and marking that book. Go on from book to book until you have made it through all of them. Then start again.

Also, I suggest reading through the books of Psalms and Proverbs along with whatever other book you are reading through. At least one Psalm and one book of Proverbs a day.

Does this sound like a lot of reading?

Maybe at first. But I think you will soon be like me and look forward with anticipation to your Bible reading each day.

Now, here is a **key** to being transformed. As you read and mark the Bible, book by book, pray the Scriptures back to God. They are His Word and His Word is true.

A lot of people don't know how to pray but if you simply pray back God's Word to Him as you read through the Bible each day you will never lack for things to pray about! Then go on from there and pray whatever else you have on your heart. But start by praying the Scriptures and you will see power come into your prayer life!

By reading the Bible and praying the Scriptures, you are not only enriching the soil of your heart and mind *but you are planting seeds*, good seeds, the seeds of God's Word into that enriched ground.

Now, getting back to the farmer. After the ground is cleared and enriched, after the seeds are planted, what comes next?

Waiting!

And watering! Watering means that you keep flooding your heart and mind with the Word of God and you keep praying the Scriptures.

There is a time of waiting before the seeds germinate and grow. There is more time before they break through the enriched soil. There is much more time until the *harvest*.

> *"Do not lose heart in doing good.*
> *For in due season you will reap the harvest,*
> *if you do not give up."*
>
> *Galatians 6:9*

No change is easy. You have to WANT it. You have to WANT IT BAD ENOUGH TO TOUGH IT OUT.

Even so, we are not the ones who ultimately bring about a transformation in our lives. We may be able to change a little temporarily but we cannot actually "transform" ourselves. We don't have the power in us to do that. It is only God Himself that has such power.

Let me explain.

People naturally live their lives for themselves. They think they are the "master" of their lives and can run their lives anyway they want to.

But, **NOT** IF YOU WANT TO SUCCEED IN THE ETERNAL SENSE OF THE WORD!

NOT IF YOU WANT YOUR LIFE TO COUNT FOR ALL ETERNITY!

NOT IF YOU WANT GOD'S BEST FOR YOU!

NOT IF YOU WANT TO BE SET FREE FROM THE POWER OF SIN IN YOUR LIFE AND WANT TO EXPERIENCE THE POWER OF GOD AND HIS GOODNESS!

There is a word in Hebrew, *"teshuvah"*, that is translated as "repentance" in the English. But what actually IS repentance or *"teshuvah"?*

"Shuv" means "to return; to turn around; to turn away from; to turn to..."

"Teshuvah" is the act of *"shuv"* as performed by one's self. Therefore it means *"to turn one's self around and return"*. Because we originally come from God, when we *"make teshuvah"* we **turn ourselves around and return to God!**

This is what "repentance" truly means!

Now, when a person **"returns to God"** it is nearly always after having lived a life that is not pleasing to God, a life of sin and self. We deserve punishment for the evil we have done, the people we have hurt, the good we COULD have done, but did not do, and so on...

We do not have the power to live a life pleasing to God on our own. But God Himself provided the answer for us!

He sent His representative to this earth, Y'shuah the Messiah (Jesus the Christ), who came and took our

7

punishment upon Himself in a physical body. This DOES NOT MEAN THAT GOD DIED! Y'shuah is the *"tzim'tzum"* of Father God. *"Tzim'tzum"* means "to contract" or "to reduce". The Father contracted, or reduced, His essence into a human form in order to take upon Himself, through Y'shuah, our suffering and punishment and to set us free from the power of sin and death in our lives!

Many times in the Bible it talks about the "arm of God" or "hand of God". Arms and hands are an extension of a person. So too, Y'shuah is an extension of the Father, not separate from Him.

How do you receive the power of God in your life? How do you *"make teshuvah"*?

Examine your heart. If you TRULY want to let go of the power of sin and death, if you TRULY want to live the rest of your life according to God's purposes for your life, then you can say a prayer something like this one:

Father God,

I want my life to change, I want to return to You, to "make teshuvah". I want to start over and become the man (or woman) of God that You created me to be!

I am sick and tired of living for myself! I am sick and tired of being selfish and self-centered! From now on I want my life to be centered around You and Your plans for me.

Please forgive me for all the times I have hurt others and all the sins I have committed! I want to change but I know that I don't have the power in myself to do so.

Please come into my life and fill me with Your power by placing Your Spirit in me. Create in me a new clean heart filled with clean thoughts and right desires!

Thank you for sending Y'shuah (Jesus) to die in my place so that I may now live the rest of my life for You and walk in the blessings You have for me.

I return to You now and turn away from my old life of sin and selfishness.

I ask these things not because I deserve them but because Y'shuah (Jesus) has opened the door for me to receive from You. So by the power of the blood He shed for me I ask You to change me so I can live for You!

Thank You Father God! Amen!

If you have prayed a prayer similar to the one above with all your heart, you are now a NEW CREATION! The old things are GONE and all things are NEW!

Trust God for what He is doing in your life!

Now open up your Bible and start reading! You have a new life ahead of you, the one God created you to live!

What I suggest to you, concerning Bible reading and prayer, may sound hard but start with what you are able to do NOW. Then add to it. Little by little you will see and feel the changes that are taking place and you will not want to go back!

BECOMING "OTHER" CENTERED

"Blessed be the God and Father
of our Master
Y'shuah (Jesus) HaMashiach (Christ),
the Father of compassion
and the God of all comfort,
who comforts us in all our afflictions,
enabling us to comfort
those who are in every affliction,
through the comfort
with which we ourselves are comforted
by God."

2 Corinthians 1:3&4

Have you ever wondered why God allows us to go through stress and suffering? Sometimes very great stress and very great suffering?

It is because He created us to be His hands, His feet, His mouth, His comfort to others. Our calling is to be His representatives on earth in every situation we find ourselves in.

If we do not experience stress, afflictions, health problems, financial problems, family problems and many other types of suffering, we would not be able to comfort others with the comfort God has for us if we turn to Him in our afflictions and let Him comfort us. This is a high calling of God on our lives! The greater the suffering, the greater the calling.

Have you ever known someone who has gone through tremendous suffering in some way but who seems to have a deep understanding of God and His ways? And who is able to weather storms that others break down in? Someone who is steadfast in their faith no matter what happens? Someone who is at peace with God and who can trust Him no matter what is going on around him or her? Someone who, in spite of what they are going through, can keep their joy?

This is a person God has prepared through suffering and stress to help comfort others. This is someone who can help keep others focused on God and His greatness and goodness in the times of the hardest stresses in life.

If someone is willing to be used by God, this is one of the greatest ways – through suffering. Suffering, if we allow it, will transform us. It has the potential of purifying us like silver and gold in a blazing hot furnace.

When we are "heated up" the dross comes to the top. Just like silver and gold!

What kind of dross, you may ask?

Lets see...maybe anger? Maybe frustration? Maybe hate? Maybe fear? Maybe impatience? Maybe selfishness or selfcenteredness?

Whatever is not of God will be exposed in times of stress!

It's meant to be that way!

When silver or gold are heated in a very hot furnace, what happens? The dross, or impurities come to the top. They look like ugly foam. Then the one working the furnace can "skim" the dross off the top until all that is left is pure silver and pure gold!

It is amazing how God made the things of this material world to reflect what happens in the spiritual world! There is always an illustration in the material of what happens in the spiritual. This is for our benefit, to facilitate our ability to understand things *spiritual* (which we cannot see with our natural eyes). By seeing **with** our eyes something that corresponds to our *spiritual* situation in the *material* world, we actually start to develop our *"spiritual"* eyes.

This is one reason why, when we read the Bible, we should always be asking God to reveal the spiritual application of a natural or material illustration.

Now, God wants us to be able to comfort others with the same type of comfort we have received from Him in our own afflictions. God wants us to learn to take our eyes off of ourselves and think about others and what they are going through.

I know from experience, that when I am suffering physically in some way, if I start thinking about someone I can pray for who may be suffering more than me, or if I can call someone who is suffering in some way too and pray with them, it brings about my own healing...not always right away, but eventually, in God's time...

So what does "becoming other centered" have to do with being able to "wait on God"?

As long as we are centered on ourselves, we will be impatient and we will not be able to "see" beyond our present circumstances to the "purpose of God" for them.

KEYS TO BLESSING

"Every good gift
and every perfect gift
is from above,
coming down from the Father of lights,
with whom there is no change
or shadow of turning."

James 1:17

As we see from this verse in the book of James, ALL blessings are from God. Now let's look at a verse from Romans:

"And we know that ALL things
work together for GOOD
to those
who love God,
to those who are called,
according to His purposes."

Romans 8:28

God has a plan and a purpose for EVERYTHING that He allows into our lives. Does God do evil? NO...but He allows suffering to transform our character and to accomplish His purposes in our lives.

"For in HOPE we are saved,
but HOPE that is seen is not HOPE,
for who HOPES
for what he sees?

But if we HOPE for what we do not see

*then we eagerly WAIT for it
with perseverance."*

Romans 8:24&25

The Hebrew word translated as "hope" is **Ka'vah**.

Ka'vah actually means: **To wait expectantly in HOPE**.

We learn from this Hebrew word that **WAITING** is a part of **HOPE**. But not JUST waiting. We are to WAIT **EXPECTANTLY**.

Hebrew is an **action** language. English is much more passive. So, in order to understand the meaning of Scripture we must look for the action of a word.

What is the **action** of **hope**?

What is the **action** of **waiting**?

First I want to give you another Scripture:

*"I have walked in my integrity,
and trusted in YHWH (the Lord)
without wavering."*

Psalm 26:1

I think this verse gives us a **KEY** to **waiting expectantly in hope** no matter what circumstance you may be in.

Ask God, if there is anything in your life that does not please Him. He will show you.

Then ask God to help you change in that area to your life so it will come in line with His will.

Maybe there is more than one thing God is trying to work out in your life right now. Take them one by one. Don't get frustrated or overwhelmed. God doesn't want that. He is patient with us all. The key is to be on His path! And His path is a path of transformation...

Now, move forward in the direction of your hope.

What do I mean by that?

OK, let's take healing. Everyone needs healing from something, sometime. Personal healing is probably one of the most common prayers there is! So many preachers say things like, "Claim your healing!" and "God wants everyone healed!" even "Satan is the one who wants you sick!" and so on.

But I have a little different view of this from my own experiences.

Whatever we are going through, God has allowed.

Whatever He has allowed is for our good.

There is always a purpose in what we go through.

This is the essence of having **"EMUNAH"** or what is translated as **faith**.

Now, back to healing.

Do you have high blood pressure? Maybe God's purpose for you is a healthier diet.

Do you have stress? Maybe God's purpose for you is to let go of your need to control. Or set boundaries with certain people in your life.

Do you have back pain? Maybe God wants you to move and stretch more. Maybe you are sitting too long (this was one of my problems -sitting at the computer longer than was healthy for me).

Do you get headaches? Maybe you are worrying over things that only God can take care of.

And the list goes on...

These are only examples of what God **MAY** be working out in your life...He will let you know in your own specific situation if you ask Him. Maybe there is something **UNHEALTHY in your lifestyle** that God is trying to get you to change.

Now, as you **wait expectantly in hope** for your complete and total healing, obey God and what He is telling you to do!

Impatience leads to demanding. This is not an attitude God wants us to have.

You can apply this same way of thinking to any area of your life, to any stress, to any seemingly "unanswered" prayer. The truth is that God answers ALL of our prayers if we are in a relationship with Him.

Are you in a bad financial situation?

Ask God if you have made bad financial choices that He is wanting you to change.

Do you need a job?

Ask God to reveal to you how He has gifted you then start using your gifts. Scripture tells us over and over that we will be blessed by the working of our hands...

Are you wanting a child but have not been able to have one yet?

Reach out to other children and bless them. When we bless others, when we offer "sacrifices" of thanksgiving and praise, blessings will come to us as well.

Are you wanting to get married but haven't met the right person, your soul-mate, yet?

Be sure to evaluate yourself! Are there things in your life that would not make YOU a good spouse in a marriage? Let God transform those areas before you get in to a wrong relationship. Then **wait expectantly in hope** for God to bring His best to you, someone you can truly share life with and serve Him in a greater way with.

In the end of things, life is all about trust. Trusting God.

This sounds simple, but once again the act of trusting is an action word.

"Faith (Emunah)
without works is DEAD."

James 2:20

Our faith (emunah) is "proven" to be true faith (emunah) when we act upon it. Until that time IT IS DEAD, it is NOT ALIVE, it is good for nothing, it is useless. Faith (emunah) is not genuine until we put our faith (emunah) into action.

Remember, Hebrew is all about **action. Without action we do not truly have faith at all.**

So, how does one put faith (emunah) into action?

There are so many ways!

"Faith (Emunah)
is the substance of what is expected,
the evidence
of what is not yet seen."

Hebrews 11:1

*We are to **ACT** as though we have already received what we hope for by faith!*

For example, if you are praying for someone to change their behavior, don't look at them the way they are at this very moment in time, but look at them through the eyes of faith! Try to imagine them as the man or woman God is "re-creating" them to become!

If you do this, **YOUR** words and **YOUR** actions towards this person will change! **YOU** will change first!

What?

Yes. We always change when we pray. **Then** we will witness miracles in other peoples lives!

So, ask God how to put your faith (emunah) into action. He will show you. Then it is up to you to act upon your faith (emunah), **TRUSTING** God to perform His Word and never giving up **HOPE**!

EXAMPLES OF *IMPATIENCE* FROM SCRIPTURE

**"And all these came upon them as examples,
and they were written
as a warning to us,
on whom the ends of the ages
have come,
so that he who thinks he stands,
take heed
so he will not fall."**

1 Corinthians 10:11&12

We are so very blessed to have the Scriptures! If we, not only read them, but study them, we will gain wisdom for life. They have been written to help us avoid mistakes others have made. They were written to warn us of the consequences of sin and evil. We do ourselves a great service, and our families too, by learning from studying the Scriptures for ourselves.

There are examples in Scripture concerning every and any situation of life. They may not be EXACTLY what we are going through but they illustrate the PRINCIPLES of living life in such a way that we will receive God's blessings. It is up to us to learn to apply them to our own specific situations.

Sometimes we need help from others, or just an "outside" opinion about something, this is where DISCIPLESHIP is of utmost importance. But, unfortunately, discipleship is very lacking in the Christian world. *(My books are designed to help with this lack.)*

Here are a few examples from Scripture about the

consequences of being *IMPATIENT*, of not waiting for God.

The first is the well known example of Abraham and Sarah. Abraham is known for his faith. He is called "the father of faith"! His faith was "accounted to him as righteousness"!

But, like all of us, he had times of weakness and doubt.

It is easy for us to read Scripture and ask, "How could they do **such and such** after all God had done for them?" But wait! What does the Scripture from 1 Corinthians 10 say?

> *"...so he that thinks he stands*
> *take heed*
> *so he will not fall."*

Whenever we are tempted to point our finger at someone for something, we do well to stop and consider our own words, actions and attitudes first!

Take heed so we will not fall!

Abraham and Sarah were very old when God first promised Abraham that he would have more descendants "as the dust of the earth".

Sometimes when God gives us a promise we must wait for that promise to become reality. Why? Maybe so our trust in God will become stronger as we persevere in prayer for the promise to transpire. Maybe we need some work on our character before we will be ready to receive the promise and not misappropriate it.

No matter, if there is a time of waiting, it is an important, necessary time.

Sarah began to doubt God. Oftentimes impatience begins this way, with doubting in either the goodness or the greatness of God and His promises. Her doubts and impatience transferred to Abraham and he ended up sinning with Sarah's maid servant, Hagar. Ishmael was born and ever since there has been strife between the descendants of Ishmael and the descendants of his half brother Isaac.

Not only that. Perhaps they would not have had to *wait another thirteen years* before Isaac was born! Perhaps God was just about to announce his promised son's *soon-coming* birth!

There is a saying that *it's always darkest before the dawn!* No matter how long you have been waiting on God for something, dawn will come! Don't let doubts lead to impatience for in the end you will no doubt regret not waiting.

This one act of impatience on the part of Abraham, has affected millions of people! And not for the good…

Then who can forget the story of the impatience of the Israelite people when Moses went up on Mt. Sinai? When they actually turned away from YHWH (the Lord), who had just rescued them from their slavery in Egypt, and began to worship a golden calf?

*"How quickly
they forgot His works,
and would not wait
for His counsel."*

Psalm 106:13

Moses had been gone for a month. Doubts began to enter the minds and hearts of the people. Not all of the people but a great many of them. In their doubts they turned to idol worship.

Now, before we point fingers, think about this. If you get discouraged, if things are not turning out how YOU had hoped, do you go shopping? Do you buy yourself a new car or boat? Do you complain and nag those around you? If so, you have just turned your focus off of God and His will. You have just turned to an "idol" to fill the void you feel. If we are not diligent in serving God we will eventually fall into serving our "idols", whether it be someone or something other than God.

Another infamous example of impatience as recorded in Scripture is concerning King Saul, the first king of Israel. The story is in 1 Samuel 13. King Saul and the Israelites were engaged in fighting the Philistines. The battles were fierce and the Israelites needed to know God was on their side. They needed spiritual strengthening. The prophet Samuel was on his way to Gilgal, where King Saul was waiting, to "draw near" to God through sacrificing offerings to Him along with prayer for the Israelite people and success in their battles.

King Saul was told that Samuel would be coming in seven days. But he became impatient. On the seventh day he did not see Samuel coming so he went against God's command and decided to do the sacrificing himself.

Impatience and pride got the best of King Saul.

Samuel showed up and saw what King Saul had done. He told the king that for his foolishness in not guarding the commands of God by keeping them, the throne of the kingdom of Israel would be taken away from him and his entire family line.

Look at these examples of "not waiting on God".

Did impatience benefit anyone?

In fact, impatience, even one act of impatience ended up affecting the people involved for the rest of their lives!

This is something to really think about.

Now let's see what happens if a person resists becoming self-centered and keeps focused on God under very trying circumstances...

SCRIPTURAL EXAMPLES
OF *WAITING ON GOD*

"YHWH (the Lord)
is good to those WAITING for Him,
to those
who seek Him.

It is good
to WAIT SILENTLY
for the deliverance of YHWH (the Lord)!"

Lamentations 3:25&26

It is hard enough to **WAIT**, but we are told to **WAIT SILENTLY**...

What does this mean?

We can only **wait in silence** if we have *complete assurance* that YHWH, the God of all Creation, will indeed do according to what He has said in His Word, the Bible. When we trust God to the point that we are confident He will perform His Word, only then will His **SHALOM**, His **PEACE**, come upon us in the difficult times in life.

The Hebrew word *"shalom"* is translated in the English as *"peace"*, but it means much more than *JUST* peace as we imagine it.

The word *"shalom"* is used in the way Hebrew speakers greet one another.

In English people ask, "How are you?"

In Hebrew they ask, *"What is your shalom (peace)?"*

They say, *"Ma'SHLOM chah?"* to a man or *"Ma'SHLOM ech?"* to a woman.

SHALOM means:

> *health, well-being, condition of your life, success, comfort, peace, soundness, completeness*

If we live a life of **SHALOM** we truly have everything we need to be satisfied. This is God's will for all of us. One of His names is *"Sar Shalom"* or *"Prince of Peace".*

Only if we learn to *WAIT SILENTLY* for God will we learn the secret of living a life of **SHALOM**, wholeness and peace.

> *"May those who trust in You rejoice!*
>
> *Let them forever shout for joy!*
>
> *You shelter them,*
> *and those who love Your name*
> *celebrate!*
>
> *You surround them with favor*
> *as with a shield!"*
>
> *Psalm 5:11&12*

There are some good examples in the Scriptures of how we are blessed when we *wait on God.*

Even under the most difficult circumstances!

Let's look at the life of Joseph.

Joseph learned about **waiting on God** in a very difficult way. Sometimes we go through situations that are hard to understand. I know this from my own experience of being thrown off a horse when I was fourteen years old. Why would God allow me to suffer through a severe head injury when I was trying my best to live my life for Him?

Just like Joseph.

Joseph was obeying his father when his brothers turned on him, threw him into a pit and sold him into slavery.

What did Joseph do wrong? What did I do wrong?

Nothing. What we went through, God allowed for a reason. Looking back in my own life, I am now thankful for the hard times because through them I have learned important lessons I would not have learned otherwise.

It was the same for Joseph.

God chose Joseph for a future "role", or "mission", in his life. He gave him a small clue in the dreams he had before his trouble began. I believe God gave him the dreams to encourage him that no matter how hard his situations became, God was in control and that someday, sometime, his circumstances would change for the better.

I trusted God for the same. And in His perfect timing, my circumstances did change. My life is better now than ever before! I encourage you to trust God no matter what you may be going through right now. Have faith. Be patient. **Wait on God** and see His miracles in your life!

Joseph had to learn to **wait on God** and His timing. Think about it. He had the dreams of becoming greater than his brothers, even his father and mother, when he was about seventeen years old. But then he found himself, first sold as a slave, then thrown into prison unjustly, for no fault of his own. In fact, he acted righteously but was "rewarded" by a long prison sentence.

Was this "fair"? No. But life is not "fair". Life is to be lived for God's glory. Sometimes we go through things we do not understand until much later in life.

Just like Joseph.

What do you think Joseph went through while he was in prison? Do you think he may have thought God was being "unfair" with him? Was there any way for him to rationalize what had happened to him? Perhaps his brothers' anger could be understood because of their father having favored Joseph. But even AFTER they sold him into slavery it seemed that things went from bad to worse.

BUT, no matter what circumstances Joseph found himself in he always did his best, and the Scriptures tell us that God was with him. God prospered him and the work of his hands. Even so, time and again, bad things happened to him.

Was it because of his sin? Was he doing something against God?

Not at all – God, in His infinite wisdom, knew Joseph lacked what it would take to become a leader over the land of Egypt so He allowed him to go through things that would mold him into the man of God he was created to become.

Here is the key – Joseph never lost his faith in God. He never gave up hope. Therefore he was able to rise above his circumstances and *wait for God* to deliver him.

There is so much to learn from the story of Joseph. I hope you will read it for yourself and learn as much as you can from his life. It is in the book of Genesis in your Bible.

There is another amazing story in the Bible about the blessings that come when you **wait on God**. In fact, if Queen Esther had not trusted in God and been willing to wait on Him, the outcome of the story in the book of Esther would no doubt have ended in disaster for the people of God.

When Queen Esther had been told of the plan to kill all the Jews in the land she did not act in haste or in panic. Instead, she called all the people to fast with her for three days and seek God in prayer.

At the end of this time, Queen Esther still did not act in haste. She trusted God and His timing. She knew God was in control and that He had put her in a position of influence with the King in order to fulfill His purposes.

When we seek God in prayer, and even more so when we **fast** and **pray**, it becomes easier for us to "hear" the "voice" of God as He "speaks" to us. Our spirit becomes more sensitive to His Spirit in us. Our ability to trust God increases as we are strengthened in our spirit.

Queen Esther held not one but two dinner parties for the King before she revealed her heart to him. In the end, the Jewish people were saved.

Remember, even in this life and death situation, Queen Esther took time to seek God with fasting and prayer.

In fact, the more serious the circumstances, the more essential it is to take all the time necessary to seek God for His answers. In such times, acting in haste, or without God's direction, can mean disaster that you may not easily recover from, if at all.

RUNNING AHEAD OF GOD

"Surely no one who waits for You
will be ashamed...

Show me Your ways, YHWH (Lord),
teach me Your paths.

Guide me in Your truth,
and teach me,
for You are God, my salvation,
for You I wait
all day."

Psalm 25:3-5

I cannot overemphasize the importance of waiting on God. Many of our problems actually come as a result of impatience! When we can't see the outcome of a situation we tend to want to take matters into our own hands and act before God's time.

This is called *"running ahead of God"*.

We live in a world which we experience through our five senses: sight, hearing, touching, smelling and tasting. But our senses do not encompass all of reality! In fact, the material world is not as *real* as the spiritual world we cannot see.

What do I mean?

How do I know?

This concept is easier for some people to understand

than others. But let me try to explain. We all have **thoughts**. Can you **see** thoughts? Can they be **experienced** by any of our five senses? No. **But thoughts are real! We could hardly live without them.**

The spiritual world is the same. It cannot be experienced by our five senses but it is real and it is a necessary part of our existence.

God is in the realm of the spirit. We cannot see Him but He is active in our lives. This is a hard thing for some people to accept. They think if they cannot **see** God, He must not be real. **But evidence of God is everywhere!**

I like to take people back to the basics.

Are YOU real?

Do YOU have feelings and emotions?

Can YOU feel it when someone touches YOU?

How did YOU come into existence?

Do YOU heal when you get injured? How can that happen?

Where did all the varieties of things in nature come from?

Was it "evolution"? NO…

There is NO evidence of "evolution" anywhere. Even though it is taught in schools, it is only a "theory" and one that cannot be backed up by evidence.

Do we have ANY "transitional" forms of life in existence today? NOT AT ALL! Everything in nature from plants to animals to humans to mathematical formulas and more, is

PERFECT AND COMPLETE AS IT IS. And everything in the fossil record showed up in it's perfect and complete form. THERE ARE NO TRANSITIONAL FORMS IN THE FOSSIL RECORD!

Why am I going into all of this?

Simple. It is important.

YOU may understand that God exists but there are many people who have a hard time understanding the existence of something they cannot experience through their five senses.

In order to TRUST God, you have to believe He exists!

"Without emunah (faith)
it is impossible
to please Him,
for he who comes
to God
has to believe that He exists,
and that He is a rewarder
of those
who earnestly
seek Him."

Hebrews 11:6

If a person does not believe that God *IS*, that person cannot have a relationship with God! Here is what it says in Psalms...

"The FOOL says in his heart
there is no
God."

Psalm 53:1

Think about this. If God is real and a person does not believe that He exists, that person **cannot** fulfill his God ordained purposes. In fact, his life will be empty in a way that God never intended it to be. Only when we live our lives for the purposes we were created do we truly find fulfillment!

Now back to what it mean to *"run ahead of God"* and *why it is so dangerous.*

> *"'For My thoughts are not your thoughts*
> *neither are your ways*
> *My ways,'*
> *declares YHWH (the LORD).*
>
> *'For as high as the heavens*
> *are above the earth,*
> *so are My ways*
> *higher*
> *than your ways,*
> *and My thoughts than your thoughts...*
>
> *My Word*
> *that goes forth from My mouth*
> *does not return*
> *empty,*
> *but it shall do what I please*
> *and shall*
> *certainly accomplish*
> *what I sent it for...'"*
>
> *Isaiah 55:8-11*

These verses are the **KEY** to trusting God! When a person understands how truly helpless he is and how truly capable God is, trust can begin to grow.

Meditate upon these verses.

If you ever feel like taking matters into your own hands, remember that God's ways are *SO MUCH HIGHER THAN YOUR WAYS*!

And in Mark 10 it says…

> *"The things that are impossible*
> *for man*
> *are possible*
> *for God."*
>
> *Mark 10:27*

When we understand these two things, that God's ways are so much higher than ours and that nothing is impossible with Him, we can let go of our need to control a situation.

Actually, there is one more verse that "seals the deal" and should truly help us to "LET GO AND LET GOD" do His work.

> *"And we know*
> *that ALL things*
> *work together*
> *for good*
> *to those who love God,*
> *to those*
> *who are called*
> *according to His purpose."*
>
> *Romans 8:28*

Meditate on these three Scriptures. Then think to yourself, "What advantage is it for me to take matters into my own hands when God is the ONLY one capable of solving my problems?"

Actually, the more we read God's Word and meditate on what we read, our emunah (faith) increases as does our ability to trust God and wait for His answers.

Think seriously about your past. Has *"running ahead of God"* ever benefited you?

Or, do you realize when you look back on a situation you went through that you ***SHOULD HAVE WAITED*** on Him? Did doing things ***YOUR*** way result in good being accomplished? Or did it just result in ***YOUR*** way being done? Did doing things ***YOUR*** way bring needless suffering and confusion? Usually it will.

The big question is, ***MY WAY or GOD'S WAY?***

Try God's way and see miracles happen!

WHY WAITING IS SO HARD

"Wait on YHWH (the LORD),
be strong
and let Him
strengthen your heart!

Wait, I say,
on YHWH (the LORD)!"

Psalm 27:14

I love this Psalm! Look what it says...**as we wait on YHWH (the LORD) He will strengthen our heart!**

He will give us the strength we need to be patient. He will be with us IF we are patient, IF we wait for His answers to our situation.

God designed us to need Him! This is so important to understand! He wants to give us His best but He cannot IF we do things our way and not His.

So, this brings us to the critical question: Why is it so hard to **wait on God** and His answers?

Self.

The main difficulty in walking with God in any area of our lives is **self**. **Self** gets in the way. **Self** wants it's way and not God's. **Self** is our biggest adversary!

Self is the black wolf that will devour the Spirit of God in us if we do not starve it. **Self** is the vehicle through which sin gets a stronghold in our lives. When we serve **self**, we are

39

not serving God.

It is not easy for the *self* in us to be patient and wait on God. In fact, it cannot. *Self* will rebel against waiting because *self* wants it's way NOW.

If you think about any area of your life that you have a difficult time obeying God in you will, no doubt, find that a desire to serve *self* lies behind it.

Now don't get me wrong, we need to take care of ourselves. We are not to let other people abuse us or use us in hurtful ways. It is actually a sin, a disobedience to God, to not protect the life God gave us as a gift. This includes our mental, physical, emotional and spiritual health.

To protect ourselves IS NOT BEING SELFISH!

There is a big difference between protecting our mental, physical, emotional and spiritual well being and serving self.

Protecting ourselves from any kind of abuse preserves our ability to serve God and others. When we are abused we lose this ability. God does not want other people to "beat us down" in any way without us putting up boundaries against it. He put up boundaries with us as an example for us. Boundaries are a good thing when used to protect the life God has given to us so we can be used by Him. The enemy of our souls wants us to be "beaten down".

Protection against abuse is a far cry from serving self!

Serving self means being self focused, elevating ourselves above others, getting our way even if it means hurting others, negating other people's feelings, fulfilling the "lusts of the eyes" the "lusts of the flesh" and the "pride of life".

Serving self makes us ugly.

"Consider yourselves completely dead
to sin,
but alive to God
in Messiah Y'shuah our Master (Lord).

Therefore do not let sin reign
in your mortal body,
to obey it in its lusts,
neither present your members
as instruments of
unrighteousness to sin,
but present yourselves to God
as being alive from the dead,
and your members
as instruments of
righteousness to God.

For sin shall not rule over you..."

Romans 6:11-14

Impatience is born out of a desire to serve self and not God. When we *"present ourselves to God as being alive from the dead"*, we will learn what it means to *"walk with God"*.

Unless we are totally surrendered to God, we cannot have true *"fellowship"* with Him. We cannot *"walk"* with Him. Surrender means letting go of what we want and letting God work.

This requires trust.

There are three main words in Hebrew that are translated as *"trust"* in the English Bible. Each one emphasizes a particular aspect of what it means to trust.

Amayn – *truthful; faithfulness; steadfastness;*
      to have confidence in

Batach – *to rely on; to be confident in;*
      to be untroubled

Chasah – *to take refuge in; to be faithful;*
      to obtain mercy

Understanding the Hebrew words we get a much deeper understanding of the English word **_"trust"_**.

This is the kind of trust God calls for us to have in Him so we can live a much more stress free life. So we CAN wait on Him and be confident that He will work things out for the best – in His time, in His way.

WAITING IS AN ACTION

"Commit your way to YHWH (the LORD),
trust in Him,
and He will do it.

He shall bring forth your righteousness
as the light,
and your justice
as the midday sun.

Rest in YHWH (the LORD),
<u>wait</u> patiently
for Him..."

Psalm 37:5-7

Just committing all we do to the Lord is not enough. We must then *wait patiently* for Him to perform His Word, for Him *to prove His word true in our lives*.

I think it's like a cake baking in the oven. If we take the cake out too soon it will be undercooked. It will not taste good. In fact, it will not even be edible.

Our lives are like a cake God is baking. Do we want our lives to "taste good" or to be "inedible"?

Maybe when our "cake is baked" God plans to "frost" it and even "decorate" it! But all this takes time. A wedding cake is much harder to make than a plain, undercooked cupcake.

So, what do we do while we wait on God to perform His Word, to bring about His promises in our own lives?

43

We act in faith!

This is actually a very important activity on our part.

> *"So faith (emunah)*
> *if it does not have works,*
> *is dead.*
>
> *For just as the body*
> *without the spirit is dead,*
> *so also*
> *faith is dead*
> *without the works."*
>
> *James 2:17&26*

We are to demonstrate that we have faith by acting upon that faith. The truth is that we do not really have faith at all unless we DO act upon it.

Just like a mother expecting a baby. Does she just sit in the chair for nine months and do nothing?

No!

She plans for the baby. She buys baby clothes. She prepares a room (the husband is usually helping in this). She and her husband pick out names. There is actually a lot to do to prepare for a baby's birth!

We are to be like that with **everything** we hope for and are trusting God to do in our lives. If we don't, we will not be ready when our *"baby"* comes!

I think also, that when we act in faith upon what we hope for, we prove to God a couple of important things. First, that we trust Him to accomplish His will in our lives. And second, that what we are asking Him for we **really** want Him to do this for us!

Then, thirdly, as we act in faith God is able to mold us into the person we need to become in order for us to properly handle His answers to our prayers!

Think about this seriously.

If you are single and hope to find the right person to marry, what should you do? First, take an assessment of your life and see where you need to change in order to become God's instrument of blessing and support in someone's life. Did you ever think of it this way? Or do you just want to "find" someone who "fits" your "ideal" of a spouse?

Remember, get rid of "self" in order for God to give you His best – in everything. **WE** must diminish so **HE** can increase in our lives.

Do you need a job? Assess your strengths and see if you can use some skills. Do you need to go to school or become an apprentice to increase your employment opportunities? You can't expect to get a good job without the skills that go with it.

I think you get the picture.

Remember the word *"Ka'vah"?*

To wait expectantly in hope.

As you **wait expectantly in hope** for God to perform His word, ask Him what YOU can do to *"walk with Him"* as He brings it to become a reality.

This is actually HOW we "walk with Him". We act upon

our expectations, asking God all along the way, **_"What is the next step? And then the next?"_** He will only give us one step at a time.

By learning to "walk" with God we learn to rely on Him and trust in Him!

TRUST AND "EMUNAH"

*"The righteous
in his EMUNAH
will be."*

*"The righteous
shall live
by trusting (faith)."*

Habakkuk 2:4

The first Scripture above is translated from the Hebrew. The second is how this verse reads in most English versions.

Both are very similar in meaning, but I like the literal Hebrew. It gives a better picture of being settled in our "emunah", our faith and trust.

I have explained "emunah" in other books I have written, but for those who have not read any of them, I will explain it again.

"Emunah" is a peaceful state, of being settled in what one believes about God in three areas:

1) God is in control of everything.

2) Whatever happens to you (or me or anyone else) has been allowed by God.

3) Because God allowed it, it is for our ultimate good.

When we usually think of the words "trust" or "faith" we do not automatically think of "peace". But we should. If we

47

truly trust someone, or God, for something and have faith that he, she or He will do what they have promised, we should be at peace! Peace is actually "proof" of trusting or of having faith!

Emunah expresses that state of peace.

The word **"emunah"** is related to the word "amen". In Hebrew "amen" is pronounced "ah-**mayn**". That even sounds similar to **"emunah"**. In fact they share the same root word.

"Ah-mayn" (amen) means:

> **certainly; to be true; faithful; trustworthy;**
> **to be firm; to be constant; to last; to continue;**
> **to be supported; to hold fast;**
> **to believe firmly; to stand still; to stop**

What an amazing word! We say it after all of our prayers, but how many people know just what it means?

This gives a deeper understanding of **"emunah"** too. To have **emunah** means to live in a state of **ah-mayn!** Think about that!

Let me try to sum it up.

To have **Emunah** means:

To be certain of the outcome, trusting God's goodness and greatness to bring about the BEST possible result.

To live in the truth, not in deception or any type of falsehood.

To be faithful, to not give up hope.

To be trustworthy, to be a person someone can count on, to be true to your word, to believe God will prove His word true in your life.

To not give up hope, to stand firm in your faith.

To be steady, not wavering, to fix your eyes straight ahead on the promises of God.

To never give up, to keep trusting God no matter how long it takes.

To persevere in hope, to rejoice in anticipation of what God is doing.

To understand you are not alone but that God supports you.

To hold fast, to cling to God.

To believe firmly, not wavering in hope.

To desist and stand still, to realize God is in control and He will work out your circumstances for good as you trust in Him.

To stop striving, knowing you can't control anything and God controls everything, to trust Him for the outcome of all things.

Look at all the benefits of having *"emunah"*. There is a peace that passes all understanding when a person learns to trust God, His goodness and greatness, believing He will work all things together for good as we put our hope in Him.

Ask God for Him to help you live in *"emunah"* and look with anticipation for Him to work miracles in your life!

WAITING IN THE DARKNESS

"Even though I walk
through the valley of the shadow of death
I will fear no evil
for You are with me..."

Psalm 23:4

"You will keep him in perfect peace,
whose mind is set
upon You,
for he is trusting in You."

Isaiah 26:3

"Trust in YHWH (the Lord)
with all your heart,
and do not lean upon
your own understanding,
all your ways
commit to Him
and He will make your paths straight."

Proverbs 3:5

Amazing how God is…

Even as I am writing this chapter, at this very moment in time, I am *"waiting in the darkness"*. A very good friend was led by God to make something right from his past but it means he will be in a dangerous place for a full week.

All I can do is trust God and pray for him.

51

Everything I write, I experience. I realize much of what I write may be difficult to "walk out" but it is, in fact, the way of God. His ways are meant to keep us humble.

We like to "see" what lies ahead in life. We want to "know" the end result. But if we did "see" and "know" in this way there would be no reason to "trust" God.

Trusting involves darkness. It is the nature of trust.

We are told in the verse in Proverbs above that we are to **"trust in YHWH (the Lord) with all your heart"!**

Our heart cannot be divided or we will not experience the peace of God!

The enemy has, as his playground, a heart that is divided and a mind that is not fixed upon YHWH (the Lord).

"'For My thoughts are not your thoughts,
neither are your ways My ways,'
declares YHWH (the Lord).

'For as high as the heavens
are above the earth,
so are My ways
higher than your ways,
and My thoughts
higher than your thoughts…

…My word
that goes forth from My mouth,
it will not return
to Me empty,
but shall do what I will,
and shall certainly accomplish
what I sent it for.'"

Isaiah 55:8-11

I believe these verses in Isaiah are essential to trusting God in the darkness. Also this one:

"Even darkness
is not dark for You,
but night shines as the day!

But as is darkness,
so is light."

Psalm 139:12

When we realize **THERE IS NO DARKNESS WITH GOD** and that **HIS THOUGHTS AND WAYS ARE SO FAR BEYOND OURS**, we can start to trust Him for all things.

ALL things.

Here is a promise for those who ***wait in the darkness***, for God to bring about His perfect result:

"For You Yourself
light my lamp.

YHWH (the Lord), my God
makes my darkness
light!"

Psalm 18:28

So many times when I am confused about something, I go lay down on my bed to talk to God. Then I close my eyes and before I know it, the confusion is gone and I have clear understanding and direction.

God doesn't usually give me all the pieces of the puzzle! But He does give me peace, clarity and the next step He wants me to take. In fact, this is all we really need! Because God wants us to continue to trust Him.

This is the way God wants us to live, moment by moment, day by day.

Yes, we should make plans for the future! But walking them out is a moment by moment, day by day accomplishment…

…as we "go from strength to strength".

LEARNING TO "HAR'POO"

"God is our refuge and our strength,
a sure help in trouble.

Therefore
we do not fear,
though the earth trembles
and mountains fall
into the heart of the seas...

"HAR'POO" (Be still),
and KNOW
that I am God...

YHWH (the Lord) of armies
is with us!"

Psalm 46:1,2&10

We are finally here!

We can finally *"learn to Har'poo"!*

So, what does *"har'poo"* actually mean?

Har'poo:

to slacken, to desist, to withdraw, to let alone,
to cease striving

THIS is what God wants us to do!

In fact, we cannot **KNOW THAT HE IS GOD,** *unless* we learn to *"let go, and let God"* work out His perfect will in any and every circumstance of our lives.

God is trying to reveal Himself to us every moment of the day. But we often stand in the way by NOT *"har'poo-ing"*!

Most people probably don't even realize that when we are *anxious,* when we *strive* to accomplish something, when we try to do a task in our own strength **relying** on our own *"God given"* ability, we actually block the revelation of God in our lives!

This was actually a hard thing for me to learn.

I used to ask God all the time, "What is MY part and what is YOUR part?" This was very confusing to me.

Let me try to explain what He has taught me.

God is the only one who has control over anything and everything.

God wants us to learn to trust Him.

But He also doesn't want us to be "slothful" or lazy.

We are to make plans but we must leave room for God to change those plans.

We are to work with all the strength and ability He has given to us but we must realize that we can do absolutely nothing apart from Him.

We must give Him the glory for all things. We can take credit for nothing.

We must TRUST in God for all things and in all

circumstances.

If we become anxious or sick in whatever we are trying to accomplish we need to take a step back and realize we are in "God's territory". He does not want us anxious or sick because of overwork.

Ask Him what you are trying to accomplish that only He can do, then "har'poo" and watch Him work wonders!

To sum it up, we are to work with all the strength and ability God gives us but realize the outcome is in His hands. At the same time, if we feel anxiety we should ask God what we are doing that is not according to His will and ask Him what we need to change about our attitude or actions.

The truth is that if WE try to accomplish something that is in "God's territory", we will actually mess things up! Our stress will become greater and the outcome worse.

God wants us to live in peace!

What?

Yes, God wants us to live in peace. He wants our lives to be peaceful. We cannot live in peace when we are anxious or striving.

Learning to *"har'poo"* is the key...

So many people do not experience the peace of God in their lives, but it is actually **VITAL** to our walk with Him.

"Be anxious for no thing,
but in all things,
by prayer and petition,
with thanksgiving,
let your requests be made known

to God...
and the PEACE of God,
which surpasses all understanding
shall guard
your heart and your mind
through
Messiah Y'shuah."

Philippians 4:6&7

THIS is what the peace of God is meant to accomplish in your life and mine...the guarding of our hearts and of our minds.

The enemy cannot have his way with us when we are *"har'poo-ing"*, resting in the peace of God, trusting in Him for all things in our lives.

It is only then that God is able to reveal Himself to us...

Made in the USA
Charleston, SC
18 December 2016